AUG 0 6.

WORLD MYTHOLOGY

HADES

Adele D. Richardson

Consultant:
Dr. Laurel Bowman
Department of Greek and Roman Studies
University of Victoria, British Columbia

Capstone
press

Mankato, Minnesota

Capstone Press
151 Good Counsel Drive, P.O. Box 669, Mankato, Minnesota 56002
http://www.capstonepress.com

Library of Congress Cataloging-in-Publication Data
Richardson, Adele, 1966–
    Hades / Adele D. Richardson.
        p. cm.—(World mythology)
    Summary: Relates the exploits of Hades and his importance in Greek mythology and
includes some of the stories about him.
    Includes bibliographical references and index.
    ISBN 0-7368-3455-9 (paperback) ISBN 0-7368-1610-0 (hardcover)
    1. Hades (Greek deity)—Juvenile literature. [1. Hades (Greek deity) 2. Mythology,
Greek.] I. Title. II. Series.
BL820.H33 R53 2003
292.2'113—dc21   2002008463

Editorial Credits

Blake A. Hoena, editor; Karen Risch, product planning editor; Juliette Peters, designer and
    illustrator; Alta Schaffer, photo researcher

Photo Credits

Art Resource/Alinari, 4; Réunion des Musées Nationaux, 12; Tate Gallery, London, 14;
    Scala, 16, 18; Erich Lessing, 20 (left)
Bridgeman Art Library/Detroit Institute of Arts, 10
Corbis/Ruggero Vanni, cover; Araldo de Luca, 8
NASA, 20 (right)

1 2 3 4 5 6 08 07 06 05 04 03

TABLE OF CONTENTS

Hades (far left) ruled the Underworld. This painting by Jan Brueghel the Elder shows Hades sitting with his wife, Persephone.

In Greek myths, Hades (HAY-deez) ruled the Underworld. The souls of the dead were brought to his kingdom. He made sure that they did not leave the Underworld.

Ancient Romans had another name for Hades. They called him Pluto (PLOO-toh), which means "god of wealth." Pluto was thought to be very rich. He owned the treasures, such as gold and gems, found under the earth.

Hades was the most feared of all gods. People were even afraid to speak his name. They did not want to draw Hades' attention. People believed they would die sooner than normal if Hades noticed them.

Ancient Greeks and Romans believed in many gods like Hades. Gods in myths looked and acted like people. But the gods were immortal. They lived forever. The gods also were very powerful. People believed they controlled everything that happened in the world.

GREEK and ROMAN *Mythical Figures*

Greek Name: **DEMETER**
Roman Name: **CERES**
Hades' sister and goddess of growing things

Greek Name: **HADES**
Roman Name: **PLUTO**
Ruler of the Underworld

Greek Name: **HERA**
Roman Name: **JUNO**
Hades' sister and goddess of marriage and childbirth

Greek Name: **HESTIA**
Roman Name: **VESTA**
Hades' sister and goddess of the home

Greek Name: **ODYSSEUS**
Roman Name: **ULYSSES**
Greek hero whose adventures are told of in Homer's *The Odyssey*

Greek Name: **PERSEPHONE**
Roman Name: **PROSERPINA**
Hades' wife and Demeter's daughter

Greek Name: **POSEIDON**
Roman Name: **NEPTUNE**
Hades' brother and god of the sea

Greek Name: **ZEUS**
Roman Name: **JUPITER**
Hades' brother and ruler of the Olympians

ABOUT MYTHOLOGY

The word myth comes from the Greek word *mythos*. It means word or story. Mythology is a collection of stories.

Myths show how ancient people understood their world. Long ago, people did not know how to explain things scientifically. Instead, people told myths. Some myths told about things that occurred in nature. These stories may explain why the seasons changed or why echoes occurred in the mountains. Myths about Hades explained what happened to people after they died.

Many characters in myths were gods. Ancient people thought pleasing the gods would bring them happiness and good fortune. People often prayed to their favorite gods for help. People brought food and treasures to the gods' temples to honor them. Artists painted pictures or made statues of the gods.

This painting by Pietro da Cortona shows Cronus swallowing one of his children. Cronus swallowed his children to trap them in his stomach.

Hades' father was the Titan Cronus (KROH-nuhss). He ruled the gods. Hades' mother was the Titaness Rhea (REE-uh).

Cronus and Rhea had six children. They had three girls, Hestia (HESS-tee-uh), Demeter (de-MEE-tur), and Hera (HER-uh). Their three boys were named Hades, Poseidon (poh-SYE-duhn), and Zeus (ZOOSS).

Cronus worried that his children would be stronger than he was. Cronus decided to swallow his children after they were born. His children did not die. They were immortal. Cronus only trapped them in his stomach.

Cronus' behavior angered Rhea. She tricked Cronus when their last child, Zeus, was born. Rhea gave Cronus a stone wrapped in a blanket to eat instead of Zeus.

Once Zeus was grown, he tricked Cronus into throwing up the children he had swallowed. Zeus and his brothers and sisters then fled to Mount Olympus in Greece. There, they became known as the Olympians.

Rembrandt Peale's painting *The Court of Death* shows Hades (center) as a dark and grim figure. Myths say Hades became gloomy and unpleasant from living in the Underworld.

RULER OF THE UNDERWORLD

The Olympians decided to overthrow Cronus. But they needed help. Cronus had the support of many powerful Titans. Zeus freed the Cyclopes (sye-KLOH–peez) and the 100-handed giants. Cronus had locked up these monsters, and they disliked him. They promised to help Zeus and the Olympians.

The Olympians and monsters fought Cronus and the Titans. After 10 years of fighting, the Olympians finally won the battle. They locked up many of the Titans beneath the earth.

Hades, Zeus, and Poseidon then decided who would rule each part of the world. Zeus picked first and chose the heavens. Poseidon was second and picked the sea. Hades was left with the Underworld.

Nobody wanted to rule the Underworld. It was a cold and dark place. There was no sunlight, and it was filled with the souls of the dead. Hades spent a great deal of time alone in the Underworld. He began to act cold and grim like the kingdom he ruled.

Gustave Moreau's painting *Hesiod and the Muse* shows Hesiod (right) sitting with a Muse (left). In myths, Muses inspired artists to paint, to sculpt, and to write. Ancient Greeks and Romans believed Hesiod was inspired by a Muse.

THE TELLING OF MYTHS

Greeks told the first myths about Hades around 2000 B.C. At the time, myths were not written down. Storytellers told myths out loud to crowds of people.

Homer was a Greek poet who lived around 800 B.C. He told quest myths in his two long poems *The Iliad* and *The Odyssey*. Quest myths are about heroes. In his poems, Homer told about the adventures of Odysseus (oh-DISS-ee-uhss) and other heroes. Myths say Odysseus ruled the Greek island of Ithaca.

Many historians believe Hesiod (HESS-ee-od) was one of the early Greeks who told creation myths. These myths told how the world and the gods were created. Hesiod lived around 750 B.C. Hesiod told creation myths in his long poem *Theogony*.

Later, people wrote plays using popular myths. The first plays were performed around 530 B.C. in Athens, Greece. Historians believe that many myths known today are versions of these early plays.

Poet William Blake painted this image of Cerberus.
Cerberus guarded the entrance to the Underworld.

THE UNDERWORLD

Ancient Greeks and Romans believed everybody had a soul, or spirit. After a person died, the soul still lived. A person's body had to be buried after death. If it was not, the person's soul would wander the world as a ghost.

In myths, the Underworld was on the other side of the River Styx. The ferryman Charon (KAR-uhn) carried souls across the river in his boat, but only if he was paid. People often buried the dead with a coin to pay Charon.

The dog Cerberus (SUR-bur-ruhss) guarded the entrance to the Underworld. This huge, three-headed dog had a dragonlike tail. Cerberus made sure only the dead entered the Underworld.

A soul was judged after it entered the Underworld. Evil souls were punished far below Hades' castle. Good souls were sent to a beautiful place called the Elysian (e-LEE-zhuhn) Fields.

Gian Lorenzo Bernini's statue shows Hades kidnapping Persephone. Cerberus is sitting at Hades' feet.

HADES AND PERSEPHONE

Demeter was the goddess of growing things. Demeter's daughter was Persephone (pur-SEF-uh-nee). Persephone loved the plants her mother grew.

One day, Hades saw Persephone in a meadow. He thought she was beautiful and wanted to marry her. But Hades knew Persephone would not agree to be his wife. She loved sunlight, flowers, and trees. The Underworld did not have these things. Hades decided to kidnap Persephone and take her to the Underworld.

Demeter missed her daughter. Demeter was so unhappy, nothing grew while Persephone was with Hades. Demeter asked Zeus to free Persephone from the Underworld.

Zeus decided that Persephone could go free, but each year she had to spend four months with Hades. Ancient Greeks and Romans used this myth to explain why nothing grows during the winter months. Nothing grows because Demeter was sad that Persephone was with Hades.

Matthias Stomer painted *Orpheus and Persephone*. This painting shows Orpheus asking Hades to allow Eurydice to leave the Underworld. Persephone helped convince Hades to let her go.

ORPHEUS PLAYS FOR HADES

Myths say that Orpheus (OR-fee-uhss) was the world's best musician. His music was so beautiful that it could calm wild animals.

One day, a snake bit Eurydice (yoo-RID-i-see), Orpheus' wife. She died from the snake's venom and went to the Underworld. Orpheus was saddened. He decided to go to the Underworld to ask Hades for Eurydice back.

Orpheus' music charmed Hades. Hades agreed to let Eurydice go, but he had two conditions. Orpheus had to walk ahead of Eurydice when they left the Underworld. Orpheus also could not look back at Eurydice until they reached the sunlight.

Orpheus agreed to these terms. He left the Underworld with Eurydice following him. Orpheus did not look back until he stepped into the sunlight. But it was too soon. Eurydice had not stepped into the light. The moment Orpheus saw her, Eurydice was pulled back into the Underworld.

This sculpture of Charon was made around A.D. 300. It shows the ferryman asking for payment from the souls of the dead. Below is an image of Pluto (center), the farthest planet from the Sun. To its right is Charon, Pluto's moon.

MYTHOLOGY TODAY

Mythology is still popular today. Many books and movies retell myths. Painters and sculptors create artwork of gods and mythical characters. The Thomas Jefferson Memorial in Washington, D.C., and other buildings have columns similar to ancient temples.

Our solar system is filled with names from myths. The planets were named after Roman gods. Pluto is the farthest planet from the Sun. It is dark and cold much like the mythical god Pluto, the Roman name for Hades. Pluto's moon is called Charon after the ferryman on the River Styx.

Ancient Greeks sometimes called the Underworld the House of Hades. Over time, people stopped thinking of Hades as a god. Hades became the name of the place where souls of the dead go. Some religions have a place called Hades in their teachings. It often is a place of punishment for the souls of evil people.

Adriatic Sea

•Rome

ITALY

N
W • E
S

•Troy

GREECE

Aegean Sea

ITHACA

Thebes

Athens

DELOS

Ionian Sea

Sparta

SCALE
Miles
0   100   200

0   100   200
Kilometers

KEY

• City

Oracle of Delphi

Mount Olympus

Region of Attica

CRETE

Mediterranean Sea

WORDS TO KNOW

ancient (AYN-shunt)—very old

ferryman (FER-ee-muhn)—a person who uses a boat or ship to carry people across a stretch of water

grim (GRIM)—dark, gloomy, and unpleasant

immortal (i-MOR-tuhl)—able to live forever

kidnap (KID-nap)—to capture and keep a person against his or her will

overthrow (oh-vur-THROH)—to defeat a leader and remove the person from power

Titan (TYE-ten)—one of the giants who ruled the world before the Olympians

Underworld (UHN-dur-wurld)—the place under the ground where the souls of the dead went

venom (VEN-uhm)—a poison produced by some snakes

READ MORE

Hoena, B. A. *Zeus.* World Mythology. Mankato, Minn.: Capstone Press, 2003.

Nardo, Don. *Greek Mythology.* History of the World. San Diego: Kidhaven Press, 2002.

Parker, Vic. *Ancient Greece.* Traditional Tales from around the World. Mankato, Minn.: Thameside Press, 2000.

USEFUL ADDRESSES

National Junior Classical League
Miami University
Oxford, OH 45056

Ontario Classical Association
2072 Madden Boulevard
Oakville, ON L6H 3L6
Canada

INTERNET SITES

Track down many sites about Hades.
Visit the FACT HOUND at *http://www.facthound.com*

IT IS EASY! IT IS FUN!

1) Go to *http://www.facthound.com*
2) Type in: 0736816100
3) Click on "FETCH IT" and FACT HOUND
will find several links hand-picked by our editors.

Relax and let our pal FACT HOUND do the research for you!

INDEX